I Wonder What I Can Give God

Mona Gansberg Hodgson

Illustrated by Chris Sharp

CPH
SAINT LOUIS

To Rachel Hoyer and Jane Wilke for their enthusiasm for this series and for their ministry at Concordia Publishing House

With special thanks to my friend Nancy Sanders for her help editing this series

I Wonder Series

I Wonder How Fish Sleep

I Wonder Who Hung the Moon in the Sky

I Wonder Who Stretched the Giraffe's Neck

I Wonder How God Hears Me

I Wonder How God Made Me

I Wonder What I Can Give God

All Scripture quotations, unless otherwise indicated, are taken from the HOLY BIBLE, NEW INTERNATIONAL VERSION®. NIV®. Copyright © 1973, 1978, 1984 by International Bible Society. Used by permission of Zondervan Publishing House. All rights reserved.

Text copyright © 1999 Mona Gansberg Hodgson
Art copyright © 1999 Concordia Publishing House
Published by Concordia Publishing House
3558 S. Jefferson Avenue, St. Louis, MO 63118-3968
Manufactured in the United States of America

1   2   3   4   5   6   7   8   9   10   08   07   06   05   04   03   02   01   00   99

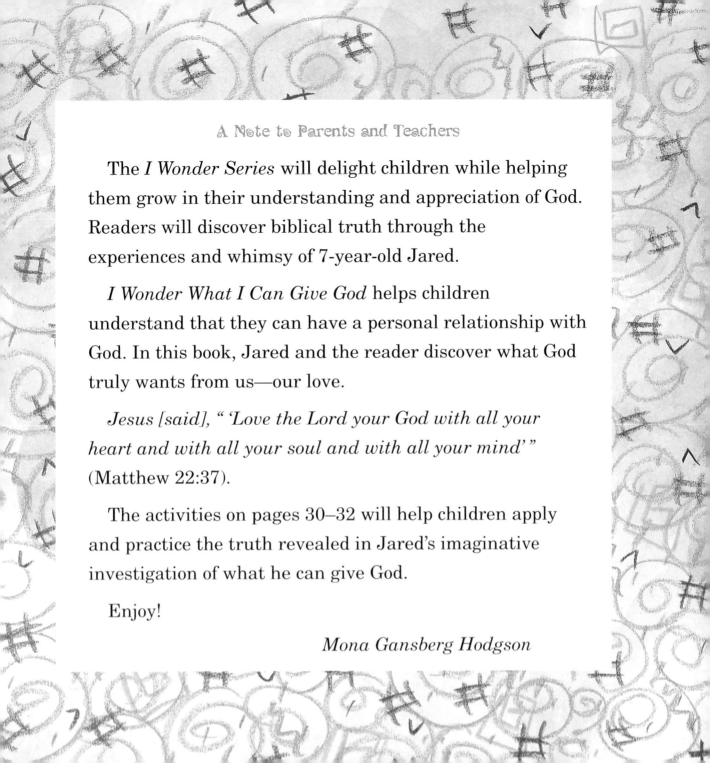

A Note to Parents and Teachers

The *I Wonder Series* will delight children while helping them grow in their understanding and appreciation of God. Readers will discover biblical truth through the experiences and whimsy of 7-year-old Jared.

I Wonder What I Can Give God helps children understand that they can have a personal relationship with God. In this book, Jared and the reader discover what God truly wants from us—our love.

Jesus [said], " 'Love the Lord your God with all your heart and with all your soul and with all your mind' " (Matthew 22:37).

The activities on pages 30–32 will help children apply and practice the truth revealed in Jared's imaginative investigation of what he can give God.

Enjoy!

Mona Gansberg Hodgson

$\mathcal{H}$i! My name is Jared. I live in Arizona.

Do you ever wonder about things? I do. Everything I see makes me wonder. Everything I hear makes me wonder. Everything I touch or taste or smell makes me wonder. Do you wonder too?

The Bible says God created the heavens and the earth. Everything in them belongs to Him. That's a lot of stars and trees! That's a lot of sky and seas!

God has given me so much that I want to give *Him* a special gift. What can I give God? I wonder. What would you give God?

Papa Ray helped me pick roses from our yard so I could give my mom an "I love you present." I want to give God an *"I love you present"* too.

Do you think God would like some roses? I wonder.

I think all of the flowers already belong to God. He made the whole earth where the flowers grow. God is amazing!

OUCH!

11

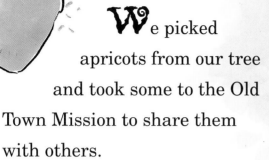

We picked apricots from our tree and took some to the Old Town Mission to share them with others.

Maybe God would like apricots too. Should I pick some and give them to God? I wonder.

I think God has all the apricots He wants because all trees belong to Him.

My Uncle Rick helped me fix my bike, so I gave him a thank-you gift. I gave him a goldfish for his fish tank.

Do you think God would like a goldfish too? I wonder.

I think God already has a lot of fish. All the oceans, lakes, rivers, and streams where fish swim belong to God.

How a si fi

meow

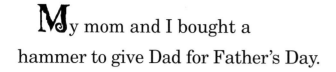

My mom and I bought a hammer to give Dad for Father's Day.

Maybe God would like a hammer for making things too. I wonder.

My dad read Psalm 33:6. It says that by the word of the Lord and by the breath of His mouth everything was made. Wow! God doesn't need tools to make anything. He is so-o-o-o amazing!

16

My mom and I baked applesauce bread. I took a loaf of bread to our neighbor who lives alone.

Maybe God would like apple-sauce bread too. I wonder.

My mom showed me John 4:34 in the Bible. Jesus said that doing the will of God the Father was His food. Jesus is God and doesn't need to eat food like we do. Amazing!

I drew a picture of Papa Ray fishing with me. He taped the picture to his bathroom mirror to look at it when he shaves his white whiskers.

Maybe God would like a picture too. I wonder. God probably doesn't have a bathroom mirror or a refrigerator. That's where my mom and dad like to hang my pictures.

For her birthday, I gave my sister a bottle of bubbles to blow in the breeze.

Maybe a bottle of bubbles would make  God happy. I wonder.

My dad read Proverbs 12:22. It says that God delights in men who are truthful. I think God is happy when we tell the truth.

What can I give God? I wonder.

Last night when Papa Ray read the Bible, I learned what God really wants. Jesus said to love God with all our heart, and with all our soul, and with all our mind.

I can give God *my love!* God gave Jesus to be my Savior and I can give Him my love in return. I can love God with my words, my actions, and my thoughts. And I can use the gifts He's given me to show His love for others.

I like to wonder, don't you? When I wonder, I think about God. I like to love God with all my heart, and with all my soul, and with all my mind.

Thank You, God, for giving us Jesus, Your Son.
Thank You, God, for loving us that much.
Thank You for being my amazing God!
Help me love You with all of my heart, soul, and
mind. For Jesus' sake. Amen.

Jesus [said], " 'Love the Lord your God with all your heart and with all your soul and with all your mind' " (Matthew 22:37).

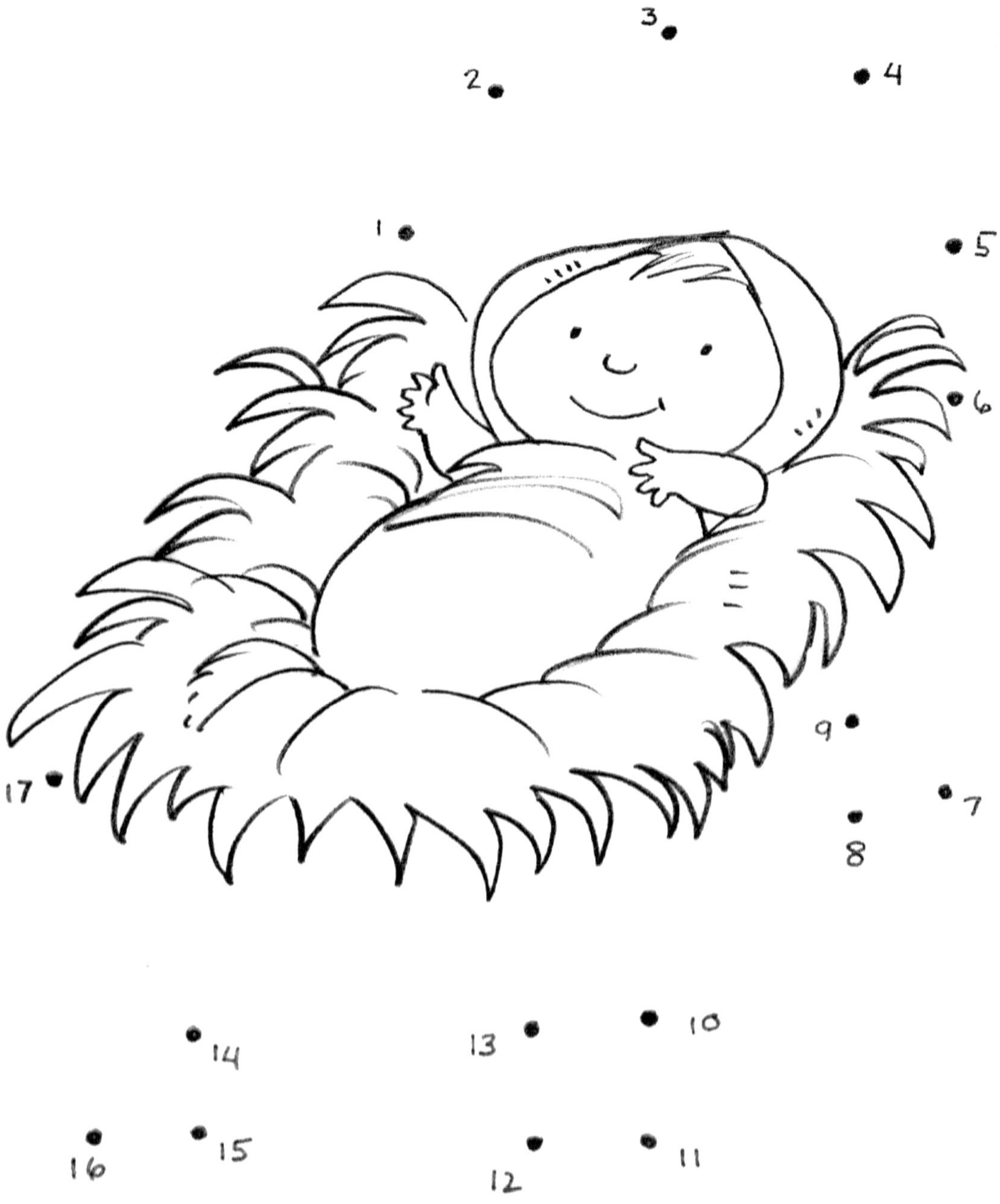
1
2
3
4
5
6
7
8
9
10
11
12
13
14
15
16
17

How will you show God that you love Him? Tell me in the space below.